LETTERS FROM GOD

A collection of letters revealing the heart of God

NICHOLE ALLEN

Cover design: Keith Brodersen - keith.brodersen@yahoo.com
Editor: Patrice London www.patrice.london.wordpress.com;
www.edenspureherbals.com
Technical Support: Julissa Ledesma- Julissaledesma2017@gmail.com

Dedication

I dedicate this book to my two beautiful children, Yavonne and Zion. You are my two great gifts from God. This book is also dedicated to my tribe, Heaven's Invasion, founded and guided by Russ Painter. To my tribe, I am so grateful, for your encouragement. Thank you, to all, who gave your time and support, in helping me bring this book into fruition. The thing, for which I am most grateful, is how you showered me with Papa's Love. Ultimately, I give all the praise and glory to Papa, God, and his faithful love.

Table of Contents

,

Foreword

Through the years I have read several books containing prophetic messages from the lord. For the most part, they were written by well-known prophets or ministers with considerable ministry experience. This book, however, is written from the unique perspective of a single mother in the midst of dire circumstances. Her very survival depended on hearing the voice of her Heavenly Father. Feeling alone, with nowhere else to turn, she called out to God in desperation and he heard her cries. He spoke, words of life and strength and healing and encouragement into her very soul. These God-messages sustained her, lifted her out of despair and brought her into a new season of breakthrough and joy.

This book contains those messages from the heart of the Father, written in letter form. Although the Lord spoke to Nichole personally, the letters in this book will greatly impact you as well. If you are in the midst of the storms of life, I believe this book will be a source of hope and peace for you as you press onward. As I read through the letters, I sensed the presence of God pouring through on every page. I encourage you to read this the book with an expectation that God will meet you at your point of need.

Although the author, Nichole Allen is not an ordained minister, a famous author or an established prophetic voice, she is well qualified to have written this book. She has put each letter to the test in her own life. In times of pain and desperation, she found comfort and provision and restoration in the Lord. She heard his voice and by faith she has come through the valley of the shadow of death. She stands today as a powerful, anointed woman of God, ready to take on the challenges in front of her. I pray that these letters will be a source of strength and healing in your life, just as they were in Nichole's.

1 Peter 5:10 (the Message Bible) - *So keep a firm grip on the faith. The suffering won't last forever. It won't be long before this generous God who has great plans for us in Christ—eternal and glorious plans they are!—will have you put together and on your feet for good. He gets the last word; yes, he does.*

~Pastor Gary Fishman
Director, Surpassing Glory
Ministries:surpassinggloryministries.org
Author, *Dream Interpretation*

INTRODUCTION

It is my ultimate desire that you are encouraged by this book. I want you to know that your life has great purpose. There is greatness in your future regardless of what walk of life you have come from, or the hardships that you have faced. Ok, now that I got that out of the way, let me tell you a little about myself

In 2012, I lost almost everything: my job, my car, my teenage daughter (who I sent to live with her father), and the financial aid that would have enabled me to complete my B.A degree in Psychology. Most of all, seemingly lost were my plans to create a better future for myself and my family. What in the world was I going to do? Never had I been in such a place of loss in almost every area of my life. I lived in a 3-bedroom town house, with my 8-year-old son. Being jobless at the time, my income consisted only of rental assistance from the government and a little child support for my son. That amount barely covered utilities, food, and some gas money for the gracious person who drove us around. I found myself juggling bills, and, at times, the electricity would get cut off. There were also times when we would have to get food from Saint Aloysius Church.

So, I go back to the million-dollar question. What in the world was I going to do? I'd pace my living room floor, while trying to figure out how I'd fallen into this season in life. On top of everything else, it appeared that all of my friends deserted me. Well, one day as I did the familiar walk back and forth across the span of my living room floor, I had this great God-thought. I came to the revelation that I was not alone. I'd always heard people say that God has promised that He will never leave or forsake His children.

As I began to trust God and take him at his Word, I started to experience the reality of His love and faithfulness. I came to the realization that I was not alone. I also gained understanding that Papa God was the one to whom I needed to open and pour out my heart. I cried out, "God, I can't breathe, I feel like my house (meaning my life) is on fire and there are no exits." Papa (God) quickly reminded me of Shadrack, Meshack, and Abednego from the Bible. These three men were thrown into a furnace, blazing with fire. After the king gave the order for them to be cast into the flames, he looked into the fiery furnace. He saw 4 men in that fire instead of 3. One of them, most scholars believe, was the Lord, Jesus Christ. The bible goes on to say that not a hair on their heads was singed. When the king set them free, they didn't even smell like smoke, and their clothes weren't burned.

Papa used this Bible account to assure me that he was with me. I began to believe that not only would God preserve me through this season, but that in the end I would see His hand of victory.

Job was another biblical character who God led me to study. Job literally lost everything. His children were killed and his finances were gone. He suffered great pain and sickness in his body. His friends who came to comfort him ended up blaming him for his many misfortunes. Even his wife told him to curse God and die. Job had no clue as to why his whole world seemed to collapse at once. Suddenly, one day God came to Job and personally revealed Himself. Up until this encounter with God, Job had always heard of God, and had faith to believe. However, after this majestic encounter with the presence and glory of God, Job was forever changed. He gained victory over his awful circumstances, never to look back!!! In the end Papa not only restored everything that Job had lost, but he also multiplied it back to him.

Although I was *going through* one of the hardest seasons of my life, I came to the realization of 4 truths:

1) God was with me.
2) God wanted to reveal Himself to me.
3) God had, and still has a plan for my life.
4) God's plans for me are much bigger than my own.

Believe it or not, Shadrach, Meshach, Abednego, Job; and yes, even I, found ourselves in difficult circumstances where it seemed in the natural that there was no escape. I came to the realization that what the enemy meant for my destruction, actually set me up to experience a life changing encounter with God. Circumstances that at the time were devastating and painful would be turned around by God to produce a multiplication of increase in every area of my life. How awesome it would be to discover the fullness of what is in the heart of God for my life and the lives of others.

This book is for those who have accepted the Lord Jesus into their hearts, and also for those who have not yet done so. For those who have decided to walk with Jesus, I pray that this book will be a great encouragement to you, regardless of the season you are in. For those of you, who have yet to accept Christ as God's life-giving son into your heart, I don't think that it's a coincidence that you are reading this book. I believe that you are being drawn by the great love of an everlasting God (I like to call Him Papa), who is determined to bring great things into your life. You only need about 60 seconds to read and agree with the one prayer that will change your life. By saying these words, and believing them in your heart, you will accept the Lord Jesus into your life. You will never be the same as you begin this great journey of getting to know God, who has loved you and known you all your life. He will forgive you of every wrong you have ever committed, and launch you into a life of freedom from anything that holds you captive.

Would you please open your heart and mind to Christ and read the letters that He has personally written from His heart to yours? More than anything else that I could share from my heart, the primary truth I want you to retain is that God loves you, He is with you, and He has a great plan for your life.

Got 60 Seconds?

It is my belief that many people were wrongly introduced to Jesus Christ. Many people, including myself, have been falsely presented with an image of a Jesus who waits for you to make one big mistake before punishing you or sending you to hell. This false picture of Jesus is not of the graceful, loving savior who gave his all to bring precious people to himself. Rather, He is so often seen as a harsh taskmaster who presents us with a long list of mostly man-made rules and regulations, that bring forth constant judgment, guilt and condemnation.

Under this "religious" system, the Christian life becomes focused on our futile attempts to prove our worth through what the Bible calls "dead works". True Christianity is about setting our eyes and heart on Jesus, the loving, merciful savior who has made us to be the righteousness of Christ, without our having to perform for Him. It is that love that transforms our hearts and minds and sets us on a true path.

Say these words and I promise you that as you give Jesus permission to come in and love you, your life will be transformed. You will begin to experience His unconditional, incomparable love and grace. He loves you more than you could ever fathom. Here we go...if you will believe in your heart say these words out loud, *right now*.

Only 60 Seconds

Dear God, I know I'm a sinner, I know I am not where I want to be, and I ask for your forgiveness! I believe that Jesus died on the cross for my sins and rose again. Please wash me clean from all my sin, my guilt, and all shame. Please come into my heart and my life. I ask you now Jesus, to be Lord and Savior of my life. Thank you for your great and everlasting love for me, and thank you for saving me, in your name Jesus. Amen!

Romans 10:9 - If you declare with your mouth, Jesus is Lord, and believe in your heart that God raised him from the dead, you will be saved.

Chapter 1
NEW SEASON

It is my prayer that by faith, you grasp, even snatch if you must, this great new season that God has assigned to your life. He has so much for you in this season. I know that you have been through a lot, but I declare right now that God is strengthening you with vision and hope of the bright future He has in store for you. I pray that you don't give up, because you are almost there. Finally, I pray that as you read these letters that Papa has personally written to you, every truth will be infused into your heart, until you begin to see the manifestation of the peace and prosperity that you were always meant to experience in this life.

God Bless You

NEW SEASON

Dear _____

      I have birthed in your spirit something so real. It's as real as the wind that blows through the trees. Although you can't actually see it, you can hear it and feel it. You can feel wind as it blows through your hair or in your face. You can even hear a brisk wind as it races on a windy day. So, it is with your new season. As day after day passes, you can feel your new season, blowing across your spirit, like a fresh spring breeze. Although you cannot see it, you feel as if you're touching it. And if you will get alone with Me my child, in a quiet place, you will begin to see it. It is your new season, beckoning you to walk through new doors, new opportunities, new experiences, and new endeavors in your life. Behold I stand at the door and knock, if any man hears my voice; answer the door (Rev. 3:20- Message Bible)

P.S. Your purpose, your destiny, awaits you my child. Open the door.

    2 Corinthians 5:17 -Therefore if anyone is in Christ, he is a new creature; the old things passed away; behold, new things have come.

8

<u>Notes</u>

Dear Papa:

NEW SEASON

Dear _____

In this new season, I want you to be free. I know that the loss, and painful feelings of defeat that you have experienced in different areas of your life, have caused you to feel like you're in prison. My child... it is now time for you to break forth, and break out of the bondage of your past. Let every hang up, and every false belief go, that wrongly told you that, "you'll never accomplish anything". Let go of every lie that made you feel, "You're not loved", or that, "You aren't worthy enough". Let those lies go! I want you to know, my child that my love covers any pain, or failure that you could ever experience in your lifetime. For in this season, I will work on your behalf, beyond what you could ever imagine. This is your new season.

P.S. I will do exceedingly, abundantly, above all, you could ask or think.

Philippians 3:13-14 - Brothers and sisters, I do not consider myself yet to have taken hold of it. But one thing I do: Forgetting what is behind and straining toward what is ahead, I press on toward the goal to win the prize for which God has called me heavenward in Christ Jesus.

Notes

Dear Papa:

New Season

Dear _____

     I have opened to you, a new season. As you have sensed, the birthing of this season has begun from within you, and surely it shall manifest. As you walk in new hope and expectation, it shall bloom and break out of you from the inside out. It shall evolve from sweet whispers of my presence in your heart, to loud bellows that shout, "New Season", "New Season", "New Season"!!!

I have prepared this new season just for you. I admonish you my child, don't look back, and just walk in. Open doors, new opportunities, and a season of prosperity have I prepared for you. So, lengthen your stakes, broaden your borders, and stretch out my child. As you walk in this new season... seek me first and all that you touch will prosper.

P.s. Move forward in faith.

Revelation 3:8 - I know your deeds. See, I have placed before you an open door that no one can shut.

<u>Notes</u>

Dear Papa:

New Season

Dear _____

    I am always with you. I have been there for you since you were born. I was with you yesterday, and saw each new thing that you experienced, good or bad. Last night as you lay down to sleep, I watched over you. As you began to slumber, I whispered in your ear my child. I made sure that you were awake, just enough to hear me and remember. I whispered a word of encouragement to you. I whispered my plans of good that are meant for you. Then I saw your thoughts. You began to question," Is this really God speaking to me, or is it just my imagination? "Then you fell asleep, but I am here to remind you this day that it was indeed my voice you heard. I want you to be encouraged in this new season. No matter what things you see, or thoughts you think, that may tell you that I have not brought about this new Season for you; know that this is your time. Don't miss this opportunity! Push past any negativity that you see and hear! Let this new season bloom like spring inside of you! Let the new life that I have endowed you with overflow, and let it be sweet to you like an overflowing river of honey. In this season you will witness, and you will know how sweet and real life is in me.

P.S. Take a hold of your new season by faith.

Jeremiah 29:11 For, I know the plans I have for you, declares the LORD, plans to prosper you and not to harm you, plans to give you hope and a future.

<u>Notes</u>

Dear Papa:

New Season

Dear _____

     I know what you want me to do, but are you willing to walk out the path I have already laid out for you? I have heard your prayers, and I know your heart's desires. Remain in my will, and don't follow your own plans based on human wisdom. Rather, seek out the path I have predestined for you. Your prayer is already answered, and waiting for you at the appointed time. In this new season, that I am ushering into your life, you must abandon old thoughts and your old ways of doing things. Trust in my word(s), for I am bringing you into a deeper relationship with me.

P.S. My desire for you is that you would prosper, and be in good health, even as your soul prospers.

James 1:5 - If any of you lacks wisdom, you should ask God, who gives generously to all without finding fault, and it will be given to you.

Notes

Dear Papa:

New Season

Dear_____

   In this new season of your life, I am taking you to a place that you have never been before. I am restoring things back to you that you have lost. One right after another, you will have them back in your possession. I am blessing you, and adding, even multiplying to you in areas of your life where you have experienced lack. This is your time of blessing. I, Papa (God), the one who has saved you, I love you. Know that there is nothing that I won't do for you. Whatever it is that you ask for in my name, in accordance with my will, I will give it to you. Step out in faith, and put your hope in me, and see the manifestation of what I will do for you.

   P.S. I will open the windows of heaven and pour out my blessings until you don't have any room left.

Psalm 84:11 - For the Lord God is a sun and shield: the Lord bestows favor and honor; no good thing does he withhold from those whose walk is blameless.

<u>Notes</u>

Dear Papa:

New Season

Dear_____

I awaken you this morning, to a new season in your life. Go ahead my child, breathe in deeply, as your spirit awakens to my presence and fills the very room. Can you hear me? Can you feel me? I am calling you, even wooing you, to walk in this new season that I have set before you. I have set you free. It is a new day. Nothing can hold you back. Now just take my hand this day, as I have positioned you in this season, to embrace all things new. For it is now, that you shall sing a new song. Yes, I will produce rivers in the desert, if needed, for you. Yes, take a step and even run into your new season, my child! For eyes have not seen, neither have ears heard what I have prepared for you.

P.S. I love you dearly.

Isaiah 41:13 - For I am the LORD your God who takes hold of your right hand and says to you, do not fear; I will help you.

Dear Papa:

New Season

Dear _____

      I know that you have gone through, what seems like a very dark season in your life. However, I want you to know, that this season is over for you. It may have been a long time coming, but get ready. Get ready to laugh. Get ready to experience overflowing joy. It's your season!!! In this new season, my child, I want you to experience new life. Let this season in. Accept it. I am even doing a new work in your heart. Experience my love in a new way, for I am completing a fresh work of love in your heart. Be transformed in this season. Spread my love to others. No longer view yourself as at the back of the line, but in the front. Receive your new season; breathe it in, for I have prepared it just for you.

  P.S. Your Trust in me shall be
      rewarded.

Isaiah 43:19 - See, I am doing a new thing! Now it springs up; do you not perceive it? I am making a way in the wilderness and streams in the wasteland.

<u>Notes</u>

Dear Papa:

New Season

Dear _____

You are being driven up into increase and prosperity, by your new season. Keep company with me, so that I can make the vision plain, and clear. Ask me what you want me to do, in accordance with my promises and Word. Speak it out, loud and clear, So that I may get to work for you. Write your request down, for I have even prepared pen and paper just for you. Be happy, that you have entrusted your heart's desire to me. Ask it in my name, and it shall come to pass. Even when it seems like it's taking a long time to come, just wait for it. My promise will certainly be fulfilled. Remember to call forth those things that are not, as though they already exist.

P.s. Request already granted!

Deuteronomy 28:8 - The LORD will command the blessing upon you in your barns and in all that you put your hand to, and He will bless you in the land which the LORD your God gives you.

<u>Notes</u>

Dear Papa:

New Season

Dear_____

    I have made you some promises. I've spoken some good things over your life. I won't let you down. I'm a good, Papa. You are so valuable to me. Day and night, I'll watch over My Word to you until it is fulfilled. You are My blessed, beautiful child. I'll always be faithful to you. I have so many good things in store for you. Just put everything in My hands. My child, I need you to see it and proclaim that It's your new season. You have been reaching out to Me, to turn some things around. I want you to know that, I've already answered your prayer. Just proclaim 'New Season', over your life, right now. It's here my child. Yes, It's really here; your new season.

My child, please do not listen to the voice of the accuser. Do not believe the lies. The truth is that You were meant for greatness. Don't let the temporary setbacks discourage you. Speak out, My child. Decree, and declare 'New Season' over your life; no matter what comes your way. I repeat. The obstacles that you face right now, are only temporary. In a little while, you'll look back, and realize that it was all worth it. Put your confidence in me, and you will be rewarded. "No weapon", I say, "No weapon, that is meant to hurt you, will be able to prosper". This is your time to be exalted. Prepare yourself, and speak my Word, and step out. "New Season"…"New Season"… Your bright future lies just ahead.

P.s. See, I am doing a new thing. Do you not perceive it? Do you not know it (Isaiah 43: 19)? It's your new season!!!

"I will be a Father to you, and you will be my sons and daughters", says the Lord Almighty – 2 Corinthians 6:18

Notes

Dear Papa:

Chapter 2
Going Through

Regardless of our age, skin color, or financial status, we all have seasons of going through pain, hardship, and troubles. In these seasons of "going through", it often feels like, we are bearing heavy burdens. Sometimes, it's hard to see the light at the end of the tunnel. I declare the peace, "that passes all understanding", over your life, right now. I pray that you grasp the truth, that this time of "going through", is only temporary. I also pray, that you will not rely on what you see, or even feel, right now; but that you catch a vision of how you are meant to come out with victory, and soar like an eagle. Finally, I pray that during this time you would experience the overwhelming love that Papa (God) has for you. One of my favorite scriptures is, Psalms 139: 8 because Papa will never forsake us. Even if we try to run from Him, He will always be there for us. Even if, and especially when, we find ourselves in hellish, places. Just hold on, you will get through, with victory!!!

God Bless You

Psalm 139:8-10: If I go up to the heavens, you are there; if I make my bed in the depths, you are there. If I rise on the wings of the dawn, if I settle on the far side of the sea, even there your hand will guide me; your right hand will hold me fast.

Going Through

Dear _____

    I knew you before you were born. When I created you, I did so with reverence. It's was a wonderful event. I, the God, of all creation, formed, and made you; carefully and patiently. I created you with the utmost care, and respect. You are a perfect work. My love for you is so great, that I sent my only son to die for you. No one has valued, or loved you as much as I have. In the world today, people assign value to you according to things, like: how much money you have, how pretty, or how handsome you are, how light or dark your skin is, how much you weigh,... and list goes on.

If anyone has ever judged you in this way my child, I ask that you please do not accept this judgment. For I, Papa God, the one and only judge, and your creator,... I say that you are a good and perfect ,creation. I have loved you with an everlasting love. Nothing can separate you from my love. Regardless of what you are going through, or how much you have endured, there is hope. I have good plans for your life, and for your future. Remember that I am always with you, and I will never abandon you. There is no place you can go, where I will not be present.

P.S. When you call me, I, your Papa, God, will hear and answer.

Romans 8:38 -39 - For I am convinced that neither death nor life, neither angels nor demons, neither the present nor the future, nor any powers, neither height nor depth, nor anything else in all creation, will be able to separate us from the love of God that is in Christ Jesus our Lord.

Notes

Dear Papa:

Going Through

Dear _____

   While you are going through the fire of trials, and hardships, I am with you. Call out to me! I will not let the things that trouble you, overtake you. I know your struggles. I know all your pain. Know that it is only temporary, and I will deliver you; and bring you into a large place. Dear child, know that I have great plans for you. I have made you some promises, and I will not change my mind. The one thing that I want you to remember today, is that no matter what you are facing, no matter what you have lost, and regardless of how painful or impossible things may seem; nothing can take you out of my hands. Nothing can separate you from my love, and, you will always have the victory.

P.S. Remember Psalms 27, though an army encamps against you, be confident, because nothing is impossible with me.

Deuteronomy 1:31 - There you saw how the Lord your God carried you, as a father carries his son, all the way you went until you reached this place.

Notes

Dear Papa:

Going Through

Dear _____

    In this season of your life, you may feel as though you are in a tiresome, but brutal battle. Weapons are being pointed at you, ready to fire. Do not be afraid, my child, for I am here. I will not let the enemy, take you out. I know the situations that you are going through; and I want you to stand in faith, for I have already brought you through to victory. Know that I will not allow your enemies, to gain victory over you. You belong to me. This means that, I fight your battles. I give unto you, my peace ,right now. My child, do not give up. I want you to stand strong, because it is I, God, who has your back. Although circumstances may seem discouraging, I don't want you to be disheartened; for I hold you in my strong hand. I am in control, and I will never, ever fail you. Receive my peace right now! Instead of accepting defeat, trust in me, and receive the life, that can only come from me. I am a life-giver to any situation. I AM the Way. The truth, is that I have the last say; and I say that, you win.

P.S. Hold on to me, despite your circumstances. You will live and not die.

Exodus 14:14 -The LORD will fight for you; you need only to be still.

Notes

Dear Papa:

Going Through

Dear _____

    I prepared your destiny, and the great purpose for your life, before you were born. Before your mother, or your father, ever laid eyes on your perfect face, I had already sown your gifting, your talents, and your purpose into your spirit; and into the very fabric of who you are. I created you to be different and unique, in this world. Most of all, I fixed the fight for you, in this life. Yes, my child, remember that, you win! Despite how things might appear, just keep your eyes on me. There is more for you. Yes, I have more for you:

More visions,

More dreams,

More heavenly encounters, and

More of my secrets to share with you.

There are hidden jewels of, who I made you to be; that are yet to be revealed.

There's more revelation, concerning my plans for your life.

There are more levels of my love to experience; more joy, and more provision.

I will not let you settle for less. Your trust in me will be rewarded. Remember, you sit with me in heavenly places, and I have given you authority over all the power of the enemy. Every time you get to a point, where you feel like you're getting accustomed to the way things are, I will cause you to hear my voice on the inside of you. I will prick your heart with these three words-'There Is More'!

P.S. You are covered with my favor; I will always bring you through.

Ephesians 3:20-21 - Now to him who is able to do immeasurably more than all we ask or imagine, according to his power that is at work within us, to him be glory in the church and in Christ Jesus throughout all generations, forever and ever! Amen.

Notes

Dear Papa:

Going Through

Dear _____

     You are not going through, in vain. I know it seems as if, one problem is shooting up, after another. Despite what you are experiencing, loss, loneliness, or even disappointment, if you would only give your worries to me, I will fight on your behalf. Even while you are going through, my love and my peace, will sustain you. Call out to me, and I will save you. I give you my peace, even right now. My child, I want you to know that your problems are only temporary. I will lead you through to victory. Before long, your worries will be behind you, and your great destiny in front of you. I love you. Trust that my plans for your, future are good.

P.S. believe that nothing can stop the great blessings that I have coming your way.

Ps 138:7 - Though I walk in the midst of trouble, You will revive me; You will stretch out Your hand against the wrath of my enemies, and Your right hand will save me.

Notes

Dear Papa:

Going Through

Dear _____

     Though obstacles come your way, do not be afraid. I am with you. It may be that every time you turn this way, or that, problems are stacked up against you. Please hear me, my child. When problems arise, I am especially present in your life; so please do not give up! Trust that I am with you. I am always near to deliver you from, and to preserve you through, anything that comes against you. Lean on me! Trust me! Reach out to me for help! I will never fail you.

     Sometimes, it seems as if, what you are going through, will never end. Your circumstances may appear increasingly darker. Please, do not be deceived by, how things appear to be. Rather, have faith, that, there is nothing going on in your life, that I can't handle. Trust me. Trust, that I will deliver you! I will comfort you. I will bless you. Know that, I am here right now! If you reach out to me, I will lighten the heavy burden that you bear. I will get you through this.

     P.S. This will work out for your good, and victory is yours.

Psalm 27:1 - The LORD is my light and my salvation—whom shall I fear? The LORD is the stronghold of my life— of whom shall I be afraid?

<u>Notes</u>

Dear Papa:

Going Through

Dear _____

     Sometimes, when you are going through, it seems like a season without end. Even thoughts about your future, can be cloudy and unclear. One minute it appears as if, you know exactly what you want to do, yet you are uncertain the next. My child, you may even be frustrated at being unsure of yourself, in this season of your life. At this time, tears may seem to come quite often, along with feelings that no one really cares. Eventually my child, you may also find yourself sitting in silence, instead of going along with the busyness of the day. At other times, you just meander through your day on auto pilot. You go through the same routine, but inside you are emotionally drained. My child, I am here to tell you that, in your time of confusion and emotional weakness, I am present to be your strength. Give your insecurities, your hurt, and your weakness to me right now; and I will give you peace and rest for your soul. Lay your head on my shoulders! Fall into my arms, and I will comfort and love you unconditionally, without any judgment. Choose to let me enter every part of your being, your troubles, and your heart. I will saturate you with my joy and peace

P.S. I will take your garment of sadness, and give you one of joy.

Psalm 91 - I will say of the Lord, "He is my refuge and my fortress, my God, in whom I trust."

<u>Notes</u>

Dear Papa:

Going Through

Dear _____

Don't ever give up on your dreams. No matter how difficult or, even, impossible, the trials you that face may seem; hold onto those dreams, my child. Don't throw in the towel. You may face times when it appears that your dreams have died. However, if you listen quietly, you can hear your dreams calling out to you. When you close your eyes, they are so real, you can almost reach out and touch them. My child, I want you to place your dreams in my care. Trust me with your vision. I will strengthen you, so that you may have the ability to overcome any obstacles that block your path. I have also endowed you with my favor. The doors of opportunity that I will open for you, no man on earth or demon from hell, will be able to shut. Trust in me! I will do so much more for you than you could ever believe. Now, receive my hope and my heart for you, which always seek for your good. Be filled with my joy! Live with the assurance that, according to my will your dreams are coming true! My child, I will withhold nothing good from you.

P.S. When you trust in me, there is nothing that will be impossible to you.

Gen 28:15 Behold, I am with you and will keep you wherever you go, and will bring you back to this land; for I will not leave you until I have done what I have spoken to you.

Notes

Dear Papa:

Going Through

Dear _____

    In this season of going through, I know that you have experienced loss. You are under the impression that little is turning out the way that you had hoped. Don't give up my child! Hold on to your hopes and your dreams! If you hold on to me, the things that I have promised, will come forth and happen for you. Sometimes, it may look as though the more you try to fix things, the more they fall apart. Put your faith in me and hold on! I will give you divine favor. The favor that I provide you, will open doors that will bring your dreams to life.

P.S. Though the vision tarries, wait for it, for it shall speak and not lie.

Psalm 84:11 For the Lord God is a sun and shield; the Lord bestows favor and honor; no good thing does he withhold from those whose walk is blameless.

<u>Notes</u>

Dear Papa:

Going Through

Dear _____

     Often, when going through troubles or dealing with problems, you may feel as if you are going through all alone. I want you to know that I am, and always will be here for you. There is no problem too big for me to handle. There is no situation you face, that is too small to draw my careful attention. I so tenderly care about you, that I have counted and know every single hair that is upon your head. I know when your heart is overjoyed, and I know when your heart has been broken. I know and I care. If you would just release your burdens to me, there's no broken heart that I cannot heal. There is no problem too impossible for me to solve. Trust me, because, there is no miracle that I cannot perform in your life.

    P.s. The peace that I give goes beyond
             understanding.

Jeremiah 30:17 - But I will restore you to health and heal your wounds, declares the Lord.

Notes

Dear Papa:

Going Through

Dear _____

     I know that there are times when you find yourself going through trying, and even terrible times. Please my child, in this moment would you put your hope in me? Hold on to me ,and don't let go. I am your Papa (God) and I have the final say. Trust in me, for I will not let you down. I am with you, and, I will keep all the promises I have made. You may even be suffering from great pain, whether it comes from a broken heart, or resides in your physical body. I am the Papa (God) that loves you, and I will touch your broken heart and your physical body. I will bring forth great healing in your life. Just put your trust and your hope in me. I will do the impossible for you. There is nothing that I cannot, or will not do for you, my child. If you seek and follow my plan for your life, I will perform miracles.

P.S. If you believe in me and my words; ask what you will.

Proverbs 3:5-6 - Trust in the Lord with all your heart and lean not on your own understanding; in all your ways submit to him, and he will make your paths straight.

Notes

Dear Papa:

Chapter 3
Feeling Low

How many times in life, have you faced situations and circumstances, that have taken you on an emotional roller coaster ride? Sometimes, life itself can have you feeling as if you are on top of the world one day; and on a subsequent day, you live under the impression, that you are buried under the weight of the world. Sometimes, lying voices from the past, may try to creep in. They tell you how unworthy or incapable you are; to ultimately, cause you to see yourself as unloved, and unaccepted. I pray that you do not listen to these lying voices.

I declare that God is touching your ears right now, so that all voices are drowned out, but His.

I declare that the peace of God is flooding your innermost being, right now.

I speak peace to your emotional roller coasters, and I ask Papa to replace all depression, oppression, and sadness with His overshadowing joy.

Remember, you are His delight, and He loves you. You have not been overlooked. You matter. You are royalty. Please be encouraged by the poem on the next page and the letters that follow.

Feeling Low Poem

Conversation between you and Papa (God)

You: Well God, I feel unworthy.

Papa: My child, I say that you are Royalty. Which will you agree with, your feelings, or Me?

You: Well God, I feel insignificant, like I don't matter.

Papa: My child, I say that you are the head, and not the tail. Which will you agree with, your feelings, or Me?

You: Well Lord, I feel unloved.

Papa: My child I have loved you, and will always love you, with an everlasting love. I sent my only son to die for you because, I love you. I set you free from the bondage of your sins because, I love you. When I look at you, I see Jesus. I don't see shortcomings, failure, or unworthiness. I see perfection at its best. You, my love, are my delight. Jesus completed the ultimate sacrificial act for you, when he died on the cross; so that you would never have to perform, just to gain the love, or approval of another. You are my beloved. You are my precious treasure. I love you, the way that you are, without ever having to perform for me.

So, I ask you, _____ , one last time, which do you agree with, your feelings, or Me?

Feeling Low

Dear_____

    I wanted to write to you today, to tell you that, I love you. I know that, as you go through life, sometimes things can get very confusing. Sometimes, you may even find yourself in situations that appear to be completely hopeless, where nothing you do seems to succeed. I want to encourage you my child, to reach out to me ,for your answer. No problem is too big for me. Believe in me. Trust me. If you find that, you have been living life, but nothing seems to come through for you, and you're just tired of it all, I want you to know that you can depend on me. There is much hope for you. You don't have to face life alone, for I have sent my Spirit, the Holy Spirit to comfort you. When you hurt, my Spirit will guide you to the truth, and show you my plan (which only is for your good) for your life. Right now, I take your emotionally drained spirit, and I replace it with peace and joy. Receive me in your heart! Receive my words, and experience great transformation, and breakthrough. I will rid you of everything that is old and lifeless. I will create for you a fresh beginning, as all things become new.

P.S. I will make you   over ,into a new creation.

Psalm: 33:18 - But the eyes of the Lord are on those who fear him, on those whose hope is in his unfailing love.

Notes

Dear Papa:

Feeling Low

Dear_____

      My child, when I created you, I spoke good things over your life. I want you to understand the words that I proclaim over you, even right now. Because you have accepted, and received me and my words into your heart, no longer will you come in last place. I have made you to be first – the head, not the tail. Many times, you have the impression that those around you, are constantly experiencing good things, while you can only sit, watch and wonder. I am here to tell you that your turn has come. My hand is moving in your life, right now. You may have some hesitation in moving forward, because of negative or traumatic experiences that occurred in your past. There were also word curses spoken over you, telling you that, you have no worth or value, and that you'll never amount to anything. You have often been made to feel that even, I don't want you. I speak to the trauma of your past today. It is over.

Receive abundant life today, my child. I touch your hurting heart right now, and I speak healing into your being. Reach out to me now, for I am the way to love, joy, and freedom. I am the truth. Don't believe the lies that others have spoken over you. For, I bring life to your very soul, though others have pronounced death over you. Lift up your head, and hear my words. Reach out for me. I have plans for your life, which reach far beyond anything that you could ever imagine. You have only but to believe, and ask. Where you have come from, and what's behind you, doesn't even matter, right now. Call out to me, and I will change your life forever

P.S. I loved you so much, that I sent my only son, Jesus, to die for you.

Psalm 16:1 - You will make known to me the path of life; In Your presence is fullness of joy; In Your right hand there are pleasures forever.

Notes

Dear Papa:

Feeling Low

Dear _____

     Don't look back to the past. Move on. There is provision ahead for you, but you must move on. Don't approach your future with your old mindsets. Expect good to happen. It's time to forget past mishaps, letdowns, and failures. You are no longer the same person that, you used to be. I am touching your life right now. I'm touching your relationships. I'm touching your finances. I'm bringing balance into your life. Don't be afraid to believe that I am making all things new, for you. Receive my words and trust me. My child, I want you to push out all thoughts of fear, and low expectations. Tell me what you want. You don't have to use a beggar's cup. I hear your prayers. I declare that there will be no more lack over you, my child. Expect good from me. I didn't bring you this far to leave you now. I'm going to do it for you.

P.s. It may happen sooner than you think. I'm accelerating the time. Expect and be ready to receive.

Deuteronomy 31:8 - The LORD himself goes before you and will be with you; he will never leave you, nor forsake you. Do not be afraid; do not be discouraged.

Notes

Dear Papa:

Feeling Low

Dear _____

Come out from where you are. I did not create you, to blend in. You are not a wallflower. You are a glorious sight to be seen. I made you to shine. Your presence, your voice, and your participation, are very much a part of my plan. Regardless of what has been said to you, or what your past experiences have been, or what others think of you, you are a person of great worth.

You were made to be noticed. Please, let your voice be heard. I know, you may have been told, that what you have to say, doesn't matter. I know that some have treated you, as if you don't exist. Don't believe those lies. You have a mighty destiny in this world; or I would not have you in it. I have ordained great purpose for your life, my child.

I know that you may sometimes, be reminded of awful things; memories of a mother or father that did not want you; or times in which, you were made to feel like, you would never be good enough. Please, please don't believe these lies. If you let my words into your heart, you will be able to see the truth. I loved and adored you, before you were even born. When you felt abandoned by a parent, friend, or spouse, I watched over you, and cared for you. You haven't gone through in your life in vain.

There is great purpose in your existence.
There is great purpose residing in you.

You were created for great things. It may not seem that way right now, but, if you hold on to me, and keep my words in your heart, your eyes will be opened to see the truth of your real identity, in me. My love for you will never cease to exist.

P.s. You are an awesome creation.

Ephesians 2:10 - For we are God's handiwork, created in Christ Jesus to do good works, which God prepared in advance for us to do.

Notes

Dear Papa:

Feeling Low

Dear_____

    When you awoke this morning, I surrounded you with my presence, but your face did not light up at my greeting. When you arose to prepare for the day, you were not full of great expectation for the good things that, the day would bring. I know my child, that there may be some situations that can make you feel empty. Whether it is a loved one lost, a broken heart, feeling like no one loves you, or simply not being able to find the right companion. I, your creator, and your father, know the struggles that weigh heavily upon your heart. I want you to know that there is no heart that my love cannot fill. My love can restore any heart. Call out to me for help right now, and I will begin to fill your soul with my love and peace. I will lift you out of this condition, and restore to you, lost time that has been stolen from you. You will come in and go out with joy.

    P.s. nothing can stop my love for you.

Matthew 11:28-30 - Come to me, all you who are weary and burdened, and I will give you rest. Take my yoke upon you and learn from me, for I am gentle and humble in heart, and you will find rest for your souls. For, my yoke is easy, and my burden is light.

Notes

Dear Papa:

Feeling Low

Dear_____

      You are always on my heart. I write you today, to let you know that, you are never alone. I know that sometimes you may be in a crowd full of people, and still, you feel despairingly lonely. At times, you may be at home, all alone, and suffer from great loneliness. I want you to know that, I am always with you, and I will never leave you. Whether driving, working, or even sleeping, I want you to know that; I am always right there beside you, to lead you, to love you, and to heal you. Whether you go up to the highest mountain, or descend into the deepest hole in the Earth, I will never forsake you. I love you so much that, I have tattooed your name on my hand. My thoughts of you are as numerous as the grains of sand on the shores. You are always on my mind.

P.s. Draw nigh to me and I will draw nigh unto you.

Isaiah 43:2 - When you pass through the waters, I will be with you; and when you pass through the rivers, they will not sweep over you. When you walk through the fire, you will not be burned; the flames will not set you ablaze.

Notes

Dear Papa:

Chapter 4
In the Meantime (Miscellaneous)

This chapter is meant to remind you of God's heart toward you. These letters can be read during any season. I pray that you are really encouraged to trust Papa and receive the different levels of His love that you have yet to encounter. I pray that you seek Him for the great plans he has for your life. Don't be afraid to pursue his purposes for you. If you do, your life will be so much greater than anything you could have ever imagined.

God Bless You.

Love

Dear_____

There is something, that I need you to know. I am aware that you have heard it a million times in the past. You heard it before, but do you know it? Will you take my words to heart, and receive what I am going to say to you; like seeds, planted into freshly fertilized soil... or will you shrug it off; like yesterday morning's coffee? Please my child, I need your undivided attention!!! Let no distractions in, right now. Focus your mind on this letter. If you know nothing else about your Heavenly Papa (God), right now, I want you to know, I need you to know this one thing.

Or maybe, you do know. If you do know, what is so strong in my heart right now; you felt it this morning, from the moment you woke up. If you know the whole reason, that I chose to write all these letters to you, then you must have sensed it all, while that you've been reading. If you don't know what I need to tell you, and you are yet to believe it, deep down in your heart; I must tell you before I burst!!! Sometimes I tell you in whispers, but I think I'll start off with a shout this time. Please hear me, and most importantly, please know that....

I Love You!!! I Love You!!!
I Love you!!! I Love You!!!!
I Love You!!! I Love You!!!
I Love you!!!! I Love You!!!!
I Love You!!! I Love You!!!
I Love you!!!! I Love You!!!!
If the yell isn't impacting
you, in your very soul, then
I'll whisper...

I Love YOU!!! I Love YOU!!! I Love You!!! I Love You!!! I love you!!! I Love You!!! I Love You!!! I Love You!!! YOU!!! I Love YOU!!! I Love YOU!!! I Love YOU!!! I Love YOU!!! I Love YOU!!! I Love YOU!!! I Love YOU!!! I Love YOU!!!! Love YOU!!! I Love

YOU!!! I Love YOU!!! I Love YOU!!! I Love YOU!!! I Love YOU!!! I Love YOU!!! I
Love YOU!!! I Love YOU!!! I Love YOU!!! I Love YOU!!! I Love YOU!!! I Love
YOU!!! I Love YOU!!! I Love YOU!!! I Love YOU!!! I Love YOU!!! I Love YOU!!! I
Love YOU!!! I Love YOU!!! I Love YOU!!! I Love YOU!!! I Love YOU!!! I Love
YOU!!! I Love YOU!!! I Love YOU!!! I Love YOU!!! I Love YOU!!! I Love YOU!!! I
Love YOU!!! I Love YOU!!! I Love YOU!!! I Love YOU!!! I Love YOU!!! I Love
YOU!!! I Love YOU!!! I Love YOU!!!I Love YOU!!! I Love YOU!!! I Love
YOU!!! I Love YOU!!! I Love YOU!!!I Love YOU!!! I Love YOU!!! I Love
YOU!!! I Love YOU!!! I Love YOU!!!I Love YOU!!! I Love YOU!!! I Love YOU!!! I
Love YOU!!! I Love YOU!!! I Love YOU!!! I Love YOU!!! I Love YOU!!! I Love
YOU!!! I Love YOU!!! I Love YOU!!! I Love YOU!!! I Love YOU!!! I Love YOU!!! I
Love YOU!!! I Love YOU!!! I Love YOU!!! I Love YOU!!! I Love YOU!!! I Love
YOU!!!I Love YOU!!! I Love YOU!!! I Love YOU!!! I Love YOU!!! I Love YOU!!! I
Love YOU!!! I Love YOU!!! I Love YOU!!! I Love YOU!!! I Love YOU!!! I Love
YOU!!! I Love YOU!!! I Love YOU!!! I Love YOU!!! I Love YOU!!! I Love YOU!!! I
Love YOU!!! I Love YOU!!! I Love YOU!!! I Love YOU!!!I Love YOU!!! I Love YOU!!!
I Love YOU!!! I Love YOU!!! I Love YOU!!! I Love YOU!!! I Love YOU!!! I Love
YOU!!! I Love YOU!!! I Love YOU!!! I Love YOU!!! I Love YOU!!! I Love YOU!!! I
Love YOU!!! I Love YOU!!! I Love YOU!!! I Love YOU!!! I Love YOU!!! I Love
YOU!!! I Love YOU!!! I Love YOU!!! I Love YOU!!! I Love YOU!!! I Love YOU!!! I
Love YOU!!! I Love YOU!!! I Love YOU!!!

I just want you to know how much, I really, really,
really love you. You are my delight, and
_____, I'm Pleased with You. You make me
smile :) You are the most important part of my
day and my night. I don't want to be without you.
My Love for you will never run out. Sometimes,
although, it actually may seem, as if you have
made your bed in hell. Still, I won't hesitate to

come to your side.

P.S. I Love You.
1 John 3:1 - See what great love the Father has
lavished on us, that we should be called children of
God! And that is what we are!

Notes

Dear Papa:

Trust Me (Faith)

Dear _____,

     I am with you. I have made you promises, and I have spoken my words over your life. I want you to know that I am watching over my word, and every promise that I have made unto you. I know that at times, the enemy, and it seems like, life itself, has come against you. There have been days and times when, you've been fought against tooth and nail, as you endeavored to hold on to my promises.

However, I want you to know, that I am protective of every single word and promise that I have decreed over you. See, I am watching over my word to perform it, just for you. I encourage you to let my words sink deep inside of your soul, so that you can see the great vision of my heart, towards you. It is good. I have a great plan of escape for every discouraging situation, that the enemy tries to imprison you in. Trust me. I got this.

Finally, my child, remember this. Although you may have waited long for the words, promises, or visions that you have received, continue to wait for breakthrough to come. Persevere ,and know that at the appointed time, no demon in hell, will be able to stop my promises from coming to pass. Yes, the words that have been spoken over you have a set appointment by me. I will not allow their fulfillment to be delayed. Cast your cares upon me, and know that your future is secure and bright in my hands.

P.S. I have taken note of everything that you are going through, and your battle is my hands. Put your Trust in me. (Psalms 10, Hab.2:3)

Psalm: 130:5 - I wait for the Lord, my whole being waits, and in his word I put my hope.

Notes

Dear Papa:

Faith

Dear _____

    My child, never forget that I, your Papa, your God, am with you, no matter how desperate your circumstances may appear. I know that sometimes it feels as if every door that you try to walk through, leads to another rejection. However, don't become anxious, for I have already made a way. My provision is already in place. There are times in which, it seems like the ground is crumbling beneath you, but put your trust in me! I am faithful, and I will cause you to mount up with wings as an eagle. As you put your faith in me, I will give you wings to soar into your bright future. My child, it is right ahead of you. I am Papa God. I sit on the throne. I am in control. I understand where you are right now. I hurt when you hurt. I love your joy filled smiles. I want you to know that, my arm is not too short to save you from the things that trouble you. Speak to the mountains in your life, for they shall have no choice but to come tumbling down. This is only a part of your inheritance. Speak life.

    P.s. Your Victory is in the proclamations of your mouth.

    Psalm 130:7 - Israel, put your hope in the Lord, for with the Lord is unfailing love and with him is full redemption.

Notes

Dear Papa:

Identity

Dear _____

    I love you. Remember that I sacrificed all for you. My desire is that you no longer settle, and that you live from my words, and my loving grace.

No more settling for harsh, abusive words that identify you as inferior.

No more settling for treatment that violates, and continually bruises your self-esteem.

I made you. I made all creation. Who are you to allow man, and sometimes even use your own, self-afflicting words to degrade you? I sacrificed my life so that you could live a full, abundant existence. Your very being is valuable to me.

Surround yourself with those who, celebrate you with love and joy. Surround yourself with my words.

 Surround yourself with those who are willing to pour love and grace into you.

 My love does not hurt; it fills to overflowing. It doesn't leave you empty. My love is warm. It doesn't give you the cold shoulder. My love won't lie to you, but will build you up with the truth. If you find yourself listening to a voice that doesn't surround you with my love, get out from under that voice and turn a deaf ear to it. If you find yourself being treated by others in a manner inconsistent with my love, a love that is sacrificial and life-giving, escape from that counterfeit love. My child, I want you to remember my words. My words say that there is much better for you. I say, that there is no monetary amount that can measure the worth of your life. You are loved by the creator of the world. There is no greater love. I put actions behind my words. I gave up my life for you because of love.

You are beautiful. You are loved. You are royalty. You have great purpose. You are worthy. You are worth of my time and sacrifice, says the God of all creation:

I am completely in love with you.

I honor you.

I lift you up, and will never put you down.

I call you the head, and not the tail.

I am so attentive to you, that I know the very number of the hairs on your head. My thoughts of you are as numerous as the grains of sand on the earth.

I provide for you.

I protect you.

I am committed to you, forever.

I'm so crazy about you; I even have a tattoo of your name. If you are worth all this, then why would you want to connect yourself to those who would treat you in a way that devalues you? I love you. I love you. I love you. There is but one thing left to make my love complete in you, just one more thing that I need you to do. Here it is: <u>PLEASE RECEIVE MY LOVE.</u> If you begin to do this instead of settling for a selfish, abusive, substitute love that will only sap life from you, your life will begin to radically change. My child, remember my words.

P.S. I love you, and I'll never abandon you!

Isaiah 49:15-17 -Can a mother forget the baby at her breast and have no compassion on the child she has borne? Though she may forget, I will not forget you! See, I have engraved you on the palms of my hands.

Notes

Dear Papa:

Identity

Dear _____

    I have great plans for you. My desire is to bless you beyond anything you could ever imagine. Keep your eyes on me. Put your trust in me. I know that you have made plans for your life that haven't really worked out the way you expected, but will you surrender your plans to me? Will you allow your 'plan A' and your 'plan B' to become a 'God plan'? I know the pain that you bear, as you have tried to breathe life into the things that you want to happen. I know how painfully disappointing it can be to have to face the very thought that regardless of how much human effort and sweat you have poured into the fulfillment of your greatest desire, it has only resulted in pain and defeat. My child, surrender your plans to me! I won't let you down. I know that surrendering your plans can be scary, but don't be afraid! I am with you. I want you to seek me, and trust me, for the great victories I have in store for you. My will is that you prosper. I made you to be a life-giver. Putting your trust in me, will cause you to breathe life-giving grace, into the right people, and into the right things.

    No more breathing life into dead situations and issues.

    No more breathing life into people that have their own controlling agendas for your life.

No more will you be robbed of life, in doing so.

Seek me, so that the revelation of the truth of what I have called you to do will shine deeply in your heart, and be revealed unto you. I promise you, it will be better than hitting the lottery. My plans do not fail and, I keep all my promises. My plans bring in a harvest of prosperity and peace. I, my Word, and all of heaven will have your back when you follow my plan. My child, I have so much for you. I love you and I want the best for your life. Walk in my will ,and I will perform the impossible for you. Put your life in my hands, and you will experience miracles.

P.s. Do not be afraid. I have taken you by your right hand.   (Psalms 41:13) (Ephesians 1:18-19)

Psalm 20:4 - May he give you the desire of your heart and make all your plans succeed.

Notes

Dear Papa:

Identity

Dear_____

      You are everything to me. You are my love. I delight in you so much, that I can't help but sing over you. I love you so much. I sing over you this day. I sing restoration over you, my child, to heal every pain in your life, which has resulted from a broken heart. I declare a prosperous future over you, despite every hope and dream that has let you down. Remember, I am with you right now, even in this season where nothing has gone quite like you thought it would. My child, there is greatness for you right here, but will you allow yourself to let go? Let go of everything that hinders you. Let go of the control, which blinds you of fresh vision. Let go of your plans. Let go of disappointments. Let go of the past, and finally, will you let go of your comfort zone? I am reforming you right now. In this moment, I am molding you into a vessel of honor. I am elevating you, and promoting you.
I know that right now it looks like you have taken a step down.
I know that right now, more loss can be seen than what you have gained, but I assure you my child, I am pleased with you.
I admonish you to hear the truth. The truth is that it is your season of promotion, right now, even though you don't see it with your natural eyes. Though it seems as if

you are witnessing the opposite, continue to trust in me. Hold on, my child. Focus your sight on me, because the truth is soon to be revealed, and will manifest right before your very eyes. I know life can become hard and lonely, but please remember I am with you as your helper. I am especially there when you need me. Try me. Engage me. Let me fill you with love and joy, until my promise comes to pass, for it is soon to come. Don't let the past distract you. Don't let your desire to feel comfortable hold you back.

I have hidden in you, treasure. It is soon to be revealed. You are about to give birth to something so great, it will blow your mind. My precious child, it's time for you to just let go. Receive my peace right now. Keep your eyes on me, not situations, or circumstances. Put your trust in me, for I am bringing you into a large place.

P.S. Put your trust in me. Miracles are to follow.

Philippians 4:19 - And my God will meet all your needs according to the riches of his glory in Christ Jesus.

Notes

Dear Papa:

Identity

Dear_____

      You are my precious child. I knew, who you were before you were even conceived. You were in my mind before anyone knew you. I made you to be great in every way. When I took a step back and examined you, before you were even birthed into this world, all I could do was look at you with love and joy. "Flawless!" I thought, as I gazed upon you with awe and love in my heart. For I knew that you were authentic, and that there would never be another creation like you, throughout all eternity. Then I wrapped you in heavenly bows of purpose, and sent you into your mother's womb. I sang over you, the day that you entered the world. On Earth, growing up, you have come to know that, not everyone was as full of the love and joy, which I have always had in my heart for you. There have been many times in which, you have felt forsaken, abandoned, or simply neglected by family and even friends.

My child, in my word, I have made a promise to you. I have promised that, no matter how old you are, or what the situation is, when your family and friends forsake you, then I would step in. I will fill the void. I will raise you, and never leave you. Throughout life, there have been many times when, family, friends, or companions, have set their own agendas and plans for the direction they wanted your life to go. At times, you may have experienced a lot of pressure as, you tried to conform yourself to the desires and wishes, of those close to you. I know that there were also times, when you experienced pain and rejection from those same ones, who claimed to love you; all because you refused to frame yourself into their mold. Some have stopped talking to you. Some have withheld love and acceptance from you. This is all because you took a stand to be, who I made you to be. I say again to you my child, I will raise you up. If your parents have neglected or abandoned you, I don't care if you are 99, I will become your parents. If your friends, boyfriend or girlfriend, leaves you hanging or leaves you, let Me step in, and fill the void. Put your trust in me. When everyone seems to have stepped away from you, and left you without support, I, with all heaven behind me, will step in and be your back up.

I will open doors, and make the crooked paths straight. I will make rivers to flow through your desert season. I will turn your mourning into gladness and joy. Your broken heart will be mended, when you allow me to raise you up. Receive these words from me and none of life's trials will ever overcome you. Let me raise you up, and there will be no pain, that will remain unhealed. Everything you need is in me, and my word. I love you. The plans for your life have been written out. Your purpose was predestined, before you were even conceived. Will you please trust in my plans for your life? Trust that they are for your benefit.

Trust that I am working to make you successful. You were brought into this world to fulfill a specific purpose

P.S I am your refuge and your strength.

Joshua 1:9 - Have I not commanded you? Be strong and courageous. Do not be afraid; do not be discouraged, for the LORD your God will be with you wherever you go.

Notes

Dear Papa:

Faith

Dear _____

I am calling you to a deeper walk of faith. Whenever faith is involved, my child, there will always be risks. Faith is a process. It is one thing to want something, that you can acquire with your own, or even, another's resources. It is quite another, to trust me with your, seemingly, impossible desires. Grasp onto faith, until, right before your eyes, your God-given dreams become your reality.

Walking by faith may not always be easy. This is especially true, when your environment and people around you; appear to paint a picture, which is the opposite of what you are praying and believing for. Please remember that, what you see with your eyes is only temporary. In the end, the truth will prevail. Do not be discouraged, or confused. I am your Rock. Lean on me. Your faith in me will produce a lifestyle that reveals your level of trust in me, even though you have yet to receive tangible answers to your prayers.

My child, I want you to think about those things that you are asking of Me. Can you, will you, change your lifestyle into one that speaks faith? I came that you would be able to have an abundant life, because with me, nothing is impossible to you. Ask me what you will, my child, and believe me for it. See what I can really do.

P.s. My Word will not turn up empty.

Galatians 2:20 - I have been crucified with Christ and I no longer live, but Christ lives in me. The life I now live in the body, I live by faith in the Son of God, who loved me and gave himself for me.

Notes

Dear Papa:

Identity

*Dear*_____

    I am your creator, and the apple doesn't fall far from the tree. I spoke the seas into existence. My vision of you wasn't far behind. I created this world with you in mind, but I also created you to be a creator, like me. You were birthed with my creative power inside of you. In my name, there's nothing you can't do. What is it that you want my child? What is it that you need? Open your mouth. Open your mouth, and speak to that mountain. Speak life where death resides. You see, I have given you authority, over all the power of your enemies. Please understand, my child; you are not wrestling against that, which is human. You are battling against an enemy, which you cannot see. Don't look at your situation, just keep your eyes on me, and declare my word.

    My words speak life over you.
    My word speaks healing over you.
    My words speak peace and joy over you.
    My word speaks prosperity over you.
    So, speak my words over your conditions, situations, and issues! My child, speak my words! Creative miracles await you. When you open your mouth,

I will fill it. You are a creator, made in my likeness. I formed you after my image. Open your mouth and speak. If necessary, I will move heaven and earth on your behalf. Change is waiting on you. Deliverance is waiting on you. Open your mouth, and see the mighty exploits that I will perform.

Open your mouth, and see signs and wonders manifested.

Your solution, the answer to your prayers, is in the power of your tongue.

P.s. Out of your mouth flows, the issues of life (Prov. 4:23).

John 15:7 -If you remain in me and my words remain in you, ask whatever you wish, and it will be done for you.

Notes

Dear Papa:

FINAL THOUGHT

My final thought for you, is the same as Papa's (God). To all that read this book, know that you are loved beyond measure. No matter what you have done, or what walk of life you have come from; nothing can compare to the love that Papa (God) has for you. Everything that you'll ever need, is in that love. Healing, freedom, deliverance, happiness, and joy are in that love. He loves you, He wants the best for you, and He is on your side. I speak, His love and blessings over you. God Bless. If this book has blessed you in any way let me know. You can find my, "Letters from God", page on Facebook, and request to join the group.

.